Guide to Hibernate

Practical Guide

V. Telman

Copyright © 2024

Practical Guide

1.Introduction to Hibernate

What is Hibernate?

Hibernate is an object-relational mapping (ORM) framework for the Java programming language. Its primary purpose is to facilitate the interaction between Java applications and relational databases by providing an abstraction layer that allows developers to work with Java objects instead of directly dealing with rows and columns of database tables.

Hibernate significantly simplifies the data persistence process, which involves saving, retrieving, updating, and deleting data from a database, without requiring the developer to manually write SQL code. This is achieved because Hibernate automatically translates Java object operations into SQL queries, while also managing relationships between objects and database tables.

Key Features of Hibernate

Some of the key features of Hibernate include:

1. **ORM (Object-Relational Mapping)**: Hibernate maps Java classes to database objects, allowing developers to work with objects instead of writing explicit SQL queries.

2. **Persistence Transparency**: Hibernate automatically manages the persistence and lifecycle of Java objects without the need for explicit code to save or retrieve them.

3. **Multi-database Support**: Hibernate can work with various relational databases, such as MySQL, PostgreSQL, Oracle, SQL Server, and many others, providing a consistent interface for interacting with these systems.

4. **Built-in Cache**: Hibernate implements

a first-level cache to optimize data retrieval and minimize database queries.

5. **Relationship Management**: Hibernate supports relationships between tables, such as one-to-one, one-to-many, many-to-one, and many-to-many, simplifying their management using annotations or XML configuration files.

6. **Transaction and Session Management**: Hibernate automatically handles transactions and session management, simplifying the control of data integrity and consistency.

Benefits of Using Hibernate

Hibernate has revolutionized Java-based application development by simplifying data persistence management. The main benefits that Hibernate offers are:

1. **Database Independence**: One of

Hibernate’s key features is its ability to work with different database management systems (DBMS). If you decide to switch databases (e.g., from MySQL to PostgreSQL), there's no need to rewrite the SQL code. Hibernate will translate Java operations into the appropriate queries for the new database.

2. **Avoid Manual SQL Code**: Thanks to ORM, there's no need to manually write SQL queries to retrieve or manipulate data. This reduces errors and increases developer productivity.

3. **Automated Object Lifecycle Management**: Hibernate automates much of the lifecycle management of persistent objects, such as session management, lazy loading, and automatic object updates. This reduces workload and simplifies development.

4. **Performance Optimization via Caching**: Hibernate supports both first and second-level caching, meaning that data can

be temporarily stored in memory to reduce database access and improve performance.

5. **Automatic Relationship Mapping**: The relationships between Java entities and database tables can easily be mapped using annotations or XML configurations, making it much easier to manage these relationships.

6. **Transaction Management**: Hibernate simplifies transaction management, ensuring that read and write operations are correctly grouped, and that rollbacks can be automatically executed in case of errors.

7. **Support for Advanced Queries**: Hibernate supports HQL (Hibernate Query Language), an object-oriented query language similar to SQL, which allows for more natural and intuitive querying of Java objects compared to traditional SQL.

Hibernate Architecture

Hibernate's architecture is designed to be flexible and modular. It is based on several components that work together to provide complete abstraction and manage the persistence of Java objects transparently.

1. **SessionFactory**

`SessionFactory` is the starting point for every Hibernate application. It is responsible for creating sessions, which represent connections to the database. `SessionFactory` is configured only once, at application startup, and is thread-safe, meaning it can be used by multiple threads simultaneously.

2. **Session**

`Session` is an interface that represents a physical connection between an application and a database. Each session is used to perform read/write operations on a database and manages the lifecycle of persistent objects. A session is not thread-safe and should be closed after use.

3. **Transaction**

`Transaction` represents an atomic unit of work that can be committed or rolled back. Hibernate manages transactions to ensure that all persistence operations are performed safely and that any changes are consistent.

4. **Query and Criteria**

Hibernate provides two ways to query a database: `Query` and `Criteria`. HQL (Hibernate Query Language) queries are similar to SQL but operate on objects rather than tables. The `Criteria` interface allows for programmatically building queries that are independent of SQL syntax.

5. **Configuration**

The Hibernate framework is configured via XML files or Java annotations. The primary configuration file, `hibernate.cfg.xml`, contains database information such as the database URL, login credentials, the database dialect (which indicates the type of DBMS), and other configuration properties.

6. **Cache**

Hibernate provides a built-in caching mechanism that helps improve the performance of data read operations. The first-level cache is enabled by default and temporarily stores objects within the current session. A second-level cache can be configured to store objects between different sessions, further reducing database access.

Overview of Hibernate Architecture:

- **Client Application**: The application sends persistence requests to Hibernate.

- **SessionFactory**: Once configured, it generates sessions for database interactions.

- **Session**: Manages interactions with the database.

- **Transaction**: Ensures that operations are executed correctly and atomically.

- **Cache**: Reduces latency and improves performance by temporarily storing data.

- **Database**: Hibernate automatically executes the generated SQL operations on the database.

Installation and Configuration

System Requirements

To use Hibernate, some basic requirements are necessary:

1. **Java Development Kit (JDK)**: Hibernate is written in Java, so it requires a recent version of the JDK, preferably 1.8 or higher. You need to install the JDK to compile and run Java applications using Hibernate.

2. **Integrated Development Environment (IDE)**: While it's possible to work with Hibernate from a command line, using an IDE such as IntelliJ IDEA, Eclipse, or NetBeans can significantly simplify development thanks to project management, debugging, and build system integration support.

3. **Relational Database**: Hibernate works with a wide variety of relational databases. You must have a running database, such as MySQL, PostgreSQL, Oracle, SQL Server, or SQLite. Hibernate will connect to this database to perform read/write operations.

4. **Hibernate Libraries**: Hibernate provides a set of libraries that must be included in the project. If you are using a

dependency management system like Maven or Gradle, you can include Hibernate by adding the appropriate dependencies. If working manually, you'll need to download the Hibernate libraries from the official site.

Installing Hibernate

Method 1: Using Maven

If you’re using Maven as your dependency management system, installing Hibernate is simple. Just add the following dependencies to your project’s `pom.xml` file:

```xml
<dependencies>
  <dependency>
    <groupId>org.hibernate</groupId>
    <artifactId>hibernate-core</artifactId>
```

```xml
        <version>5.6.3.Final</version>
    </dependency>

    <dependency>
        <groupId>org.hibernate</groupId>
        <artifactId>hibernate-entitymanager</artifactId>
        <version>5.6.3.Final</version>
    </dependency>

    <dependency>
        <groupId>mysql</groupId>
        <artifactId>mysql-connector-java</artifactId>
        <version>8.0.27</version>
    </dependency>
</dependencies>
```

These dependencies include the necessary libraries to run Hibernate and connect to a MySQL database.

Method 2: Using Gradle

If you are using Gradle as your build system, adding Hibernate is equally simple. In the `build.gradle` file, add the following lines under the `dependencies` section:

```gradle
dependencies {
    implementation 'org.hibernate:hibernate-core:5.6.3.Final'
    implementation 'org.hibernate:hibernate-entitymanager:5.6.3.Final'
    implementation 'mysql:mysql-connector-java:8.0.27'
}
```

After adding these dependencies, you need to synchronize the project so that Gradle downloads and includes the libraries in the project.

Method 3: Manual Download

If you're not using a dependency management system, you can manually download the JAR files from the official Hibernate website. Once downloaded, you'll need to include them in your project's classpath.

Configuring the `hibernate.cfg.xml` file

After installing Hibernate, it needs to be configured. Hibernate configuration can be done using Java annotations or through an XML file. One of the most commonly used configuration files is `hibernate.cfg.xml`, which contains information about database connections and other properties.

Here's an example of a `hibernate.cfg.xml` file:

```xml
<!DOCTYPE hibernate-configuration PUBLIC
        "-//Hibernate/Hibernate Configuration DTD 3.0//EN"

"http://hibernate.sourceforge.net/hibernate-configuration-3.0.dtd">


<hibernate-configuration>
   <session-factory>
        <!-- Database connection configuration -->
        <property name="hibernate.connection.driver_class">com.mysql.cj.jdbc.Driver</property>
        <property
```

```
name="hibernate.connection.url">jdbc:mysql:
//localhost:3306/mydb</property>

        <property
name="hibernate.connection.username">root
</property>

        <property
name="hibernate.connection.password">pass
word</property>

        <property
name="hibernate.dialect">org.hibernate.dialec
t.MySQLDialect</property>


        <!-- Hibernate properties configuration
-->

        <property
name="hibernate.show_sql">true</property>

        <property
name="hibernate.format_sql">true</property
>

        <property
name="hibernate.hbm2ddl.auto">update</pro
perty>
```

```
        <!-- Entity class mapping -->
        <mapping
class="com.example.entity.User"/>
    </
session-factory>
</hibernate-configuration>
```

Connecting to a Database

After configuring the `hibernate.cfg.xml` file, Hibernate will automatically connect to the specified database when the application starts.

2.Fundamental Concepts of Hibernate

Hibernate is one of the most widely used ORM (Object-Relational Mapping) frameworks in Java to simplify the interaction between a Java application and a relational database. With Hibernate, it is possible to work with Java objects and persist them in the database without having to write SQL code manually. This framework provides several features such as transaction support, session management, entity mapping, and more.

In this article, we will explore some of the fundamental concepts of Hibernate:

- **Entity and Persistent Objects**

- **Session and Transaction**

- **Hibernate SessionFactory**

- **Entity Mapping**

Entity and Persistent Objects

What is an Entity?

An **Entity** in Hibernate is a Java class that represents a table in a relational database. Each instance of the Entity class corresponds to a row in the table. Hibernate uses these entities to map data between the database and the Java code. Entities are the core of object persistence in Hibernate.

Classes that represent entities must meet some requirements:

1. **Must be a POJO (Plain Old Java Object)**: Entities must be simple Java classes with attributes, getter, and setter methods.

2. **Must have a unique identifier (primary key)**: Each entity must have a primary key, which can be a single attribute or a combination of multiple attributes.

3. **Must be annotated with `@Entity`**: Hibernate uses annotations to recognize which classes should be mapped to the database. The `@Entity` annotation indicates that the class represents a persistent entity.

Example of an Entity class

```java
import javax.persistence.Entity;
import javax.persistence.Id;

@Entity
public class User {
    @Id
    private Long id;
    private String name;
    private String email;
```

```
public User() {
}

public Long getId() {
    return id;
}

public void setId(Long id) {
    this.id = id;
}

public String getName() {
    return name;
}

public void setName(String name) {
    this.name = name;
}
```

```
    public String getEmail() {
        return email;
    }

    public void setEmail(String email) {
        this.email = email;
    }
}
```

In this example, the `User` class represents an entity. It is annotated with `@Entity`, indicating to Hibernate that the class corresponds to a database table. The `id` attribute is annotated with `@Id`, specifying that it is the primary key of the table.

Persistent Objects

Persistent Objects are instances of Entity classes that Hibernate manages in the persistence context. A persistent object is an instance of an entity that is stored in the database and managed by the Hibernate framework. Objects can be in various states during the persistence lifecycle, such as:

- **Transient**: The object has just been created and is not yet associated with a Hibernate session or the database. It has no identifier.

- **Persistent**: The object is associated with a Hibernate session and is tracked by the framework. Changes to the object are automatically propagated to the database.

- **Detached**: The object was associated with a session, but the session has been closed. It is no longer managed by Hibernate but can be reattached.

- **Removed**: The object has been marked for removal from the database.

Lifecycle of Objects in Hibernate

Objects in Hibernate go through various stages during their lifecycle:

1. **Transient**: When an object is created using the `new` operator, it is considered transient. This object is not yet linked to a Hibernate session or the database, so it is not saved in the database until explicitly persisted.

2. **Persistent**: When a transient object is associated with a Hibernate session (e.g., using the `save()` or `persist()` method), it becomes persistent. At this point, the object is tracked by Hibernate, and any changes to it are automatically synchronized with the database.

3. **Detached**: If a Hibernate session is closed, the persistent objects associated with that session become detached. While these objects remain in memory, they are no longer tracked by Hibernate, and changes are not propagated to the database. However, a

detached object can be reconnected to a new session using the `update()` or `merge()` method.

4. **Removed**: When a persistent object is deleted from the database using the `delete()` method, it transitions to the removed state.

Session and Transaction

What is a Session?

A **Session** in Hibernate represents a temporary physical connection between an application and a database. It is used to perform read/write operations on the database and manage the lifecycle of persistent objects. The session is one of the central elements in Hibernate's architecture and provides methods for executing persistence operations such as `save()`, `update()`, `delete()`, and `query()`.

Each session is created using the `SessionFactory` (discussed later) and is intended to be used for a single unit of work. It is not thread-safe, meaning each thread must have its own session.

Main Session Methods

- **save()**: Used to save a new persistent object in the database. If the object already has an ID generated by the database, Hibernate will update it.

- **update()**: Used to update a detached object. This method synchronizes the object with the database.

- **delete()**: Used to remove a persistent object from the database.

- **get()**: Retrieves an object by its identifier. If the object does not exist, it returns `null`.

- **load()**: Similar to `get()`, but throws an exception if the object does not exist.

- **createQuery()**: Used to create HQL (Hibernate Query Language) queries to retrieve persistent objects from the database.

Example of using a Session

```java
SessionFactory sessionFactory = new Configuration().configure().buildSessionFactory();
Session session = sessionFactory.openSession();
Transaction transaction = null;

try {
```

```
    transaction = session.beginTransaction();

    User user = new User();
    user.setName("Mario Rossi");

user.setEmail("mario.rossi@example.com");

    session.save(user);
    transaction.commit();
} catch (Exception e) {
    if (transaction != null) {
        transaction.rollback();
    }
    e.printStackTrace();
} finally {
    session.close();
}
```

In this example, we create a new session using `sessionFactory`, start a transaction with `session.beginTransaction()`, create a new `User` object, persist it to the database with `session.save(user)`, and finally commit the transaction with `transaction.commit()`. If an error occurs during the process, the transaction is rolled back using `transaction.rollback()`.

What is a Transaction?

A **Transaction** in Hibernate represents an atomic unit of work that can either be committed or rolled back. Transactions ensure that persistence operations are executed safely and that changes to the database are consistent. If a transaction is completed successfully, the changes are committed. In case of an error, the transaction can be rolled back to restore the previous state of the database.

Hibernate manages transactions using the Java Transaction API (JTA) or JDBC transaction API.

Example of transaction management in Hibernate:

```java
Transaction transaction = null;

try {
    transaction = session.beginTransaction();
    // Persistence operations here
    transaction.commit();
} catch (Exception e) {
    if (transaction != null) {
        transaction.rollback();
    }
    e.printStackTrace();
```

```
}
```

In this code snippet, we start a transaction with `session.beginTransaction()`, perform persistence operations, and then commit the transaction with `transaction.commit()`. If an exception occurs, the transaction is rolled back with `transaction.rollback()`.

Hibernate SessionFactory

What is SessionFactory?

The **SessionFactory** is an instance used to create `Session` objects. It is the starting point for configuring and initializing Hibernate. The `SessionFactory` is created only once during the application's startup and is used to open multiple sessions throughout the application's lifecycle. Once the `SessionFactory` is created, sessions can be opened and closed repeatedly, as the `SessionFactory` is thread-safe.

The `SessionFactory` is responsible for managing database connection resources and other related resources.

Example of creating a SessionFactory

```java
SessionFactory sessionFactory = new Configuration().configure().buildSessionFactory();
```

In this example, we use the `Configuration` class to read the `hibernate.cfg.xml` configuration file and build the `SessionFactory`.

Role of SessionFactory

- **Hibernate Initialization**: The `SessionFactory` reads the configuration file and builds an instance that can be used to create sessions.

- **Connection Management**: Provides the necessary resources to open sessions and maintain connections to the database.

- **Caching**: Hibernate supports an integrated caching system. The first level of cache is managed by sessions, while the second level of cache is managed by the `SessionFactory`.

Entity Mapping

Mapping in Hibernate

Mapping in Hibernate defines how Java classes (entities) are mapped to database tables. Hibernate offers two main modes of mapping:

- **Mapping via annotations**: Annotations are added directly to the Java classes to indicate how attributes should be mapped to database columns.

- **Mapping via XML files**: A separate XML file defines the mapping between Java entities and database tables. Although this method is still supported, using annotations is more common in modern Hibernate versions.

Mapping via Annotations

Annotations are the simplest and most readable way to map classes in Hibernate. Some of the most common annotations are:

- `@Entity`: Indicates that the class is an entity and will be mapped to a database table.

- `@Id`: Specifies that an attribute represents the primary key of the table.

- `@GeneratedValue`: Indicates that the ID

will be automatically generated by the database or Hibernate.

- `@Column`: Specifies additional details about column mapping, such as the column name and its properties

.

Example of using annotations for mapping:

```java
@Entity

public class User {

    @Id

    @GeneratedValue(strategy = GenerationType.IDENTITY)

    private Long id;


    @Column(name = "user_name", nullable = false)
```

```
    private String name;

    private String email;
}
```

In this example, the `User` entity is annotated to map its attributes to a table. The `@GeneratedValue` annotation is used to specify that the `id` attribute is an auto-incremented value in the database, while the `@Column` annotation is used to specify the column name and additional properties.

Mapping Relationships

Hibernate allows us to define relationships between entities. Common relationships include:

- **One-to-One**: One instance of an entity

is associated with one instance of another entity.

- **One-to-Many**: One instance of an entity is associated with multiple instances of another entity.

- **Many-to-One**: Multiple instances of an entity are associated with one instance of another entity.

- **Many-to-Many**: Multiple instances of one entity are associated with multiple instances of another entity.

Each of these relationships can be mapped using annotations like `@OneToOne`, `@OneToMany`, `@ManyToOne`, and `@ManyToMany`.

Example of a one-to-many relationship:

```java

@Entity
```

```
public class User {
   @Id
   @GeneratedValue(strategy =
GenerationType.IDENTITY)
   private Long id;
   private String name;
   private String email;

   @OneToMany(mappedBy = "user",
cascade = CascadeType.ALL)
   private List<Order> orders = new
ArrayList<>();
}

@Entity
public class Order {
   @Id
   @GeneratedValue(strategy =
GenerationType.IDENTITY)
```

```
    private Long id;

    private String orderNumber;


    @ManyToOne

    @JoinColumn(name = "user_id")

    private User user;

}
```

In this example, the `User` entity is related to the `Order` entity in a one-to-many relationship. The `orders` list in the `User` class stores all the orders placed by the user, while the `user` attribute in the `Order` class refers to the user who placed the order.

Understanding the fundamental concepts of Hibernate, such as entities, sessions, transactions, and mapping, is essential for effectively using this powerful ORM framework. Hibernate simplifies database interactions in Java applications, allowing developers to focus on the business logic rather than writing complex SQL queries. By mastering these concepts, developers can efficiently manage data persistence and relationships in a relational database using Hibernate.

3.Hibernate Entity Mapping

Hibernate is an ORM (Object-Relational Mapping) framework that simplifies interaction between Java applications and relational databases. The central element of Hibernate is **entity mapping**, which links Java classes (entities) to database tables, allowing data manipulation using objects instead of raw SQL.

In this article, we will focus on the following aspects of entity mapping in Hibernate:

- XML-based mapping

- Annotation-based mapping

- Association types: One-to-One, One-to-Many, Many-to-One, Many-to-Many

XML-Based Mapping

Historically, Hibernate used XML files to define the mapping between Java classes and database tables. This method is still supported, although the use of annotations has become the standard. XML files offer a clear separation between application logic and database configuration, which can be beneficial in certain contexts.

Structure of an XML Mapping File

XML mapping files follow a precise structure and use the DTD (Document Type Definition) format to describe relationships between classes and tables. An XML mapping file is associated with a class and can describe details of its properties, primary keys, columns, and relationships with other entities.

Here's an example of an XML mapping file for a `User` class:

```xml
```

```xml
<?xml version="1.0"?>

<!DOCTYPE hibernate-mapping PUBLIC
"-//Hibernate/Hibernate Mapping DTD
3.0//EN"


"http://hibernate.sourceforge.net/hibernate-
mapping-3.0.dtd">

<hibernate-mapping>

   <class name="com.example.entity.User"
table="users">

       <!-- Primary Key Definition -->

       <id name="id" column="id"
type="long">

           <generator class="native"/>

       </id>


       <!-- Property Mapping -->

       <property name="name" column="name"
type="string"/>

       <property name="email"
column="email" type="string"/>
```

```
        <!-- Relationships and other
configurations -->

    </class>

</hibernate-mapping>
```

Key Elements of the XML Mapping File

1. **hibernate-mapping**: The root element that defines the mapping.

2. **class**: Defines a Java class (`com.example.entity.User`) and maps it to a database table (`users`).

3. **id**: Defines the table's primary key and how it is generated. In this example, `native` means Hibernate will use the database's native strategy (e.g., `auto_increment` in MySQL).

4. **property**: Maps class attributes to table columns.

Example of One-to-One Relationship Mapping in XML

Suppose we have two classes: `User` and `Profile`, where a user has an associated profile in a one-to-one relationship. Here's how to map this relationship in XML:

`User` class:

```xml
<hibernate-mapping>
    <class name="com.example.entity.User" table="users">
        <id name="id" column="id" type="long">
            <generator class="native"/>
        </id>
        <property name="name" column="name" type="string"/>
```

```
        <property name="email"
column="email" type="string"/>

        <!-- One-to-One mapping with the
Profile class -->

        <one-to-one name="profile"
class="com.example.entity.Profile"/>

    </class>

</hibernate-mapping>
```

`Profile` class:

```xml
<hibernate-mapping>

    <class name="com.example.entity.Profile"
table="profiles">

        <id name="id" column="id"
type="long">

            <generator class="foreign">

                <param
```

```
name="property">user</param>

            </generator>

        </id>

        <property name="biography"
column="biography" type="string"/>


        <!-- Inverse relationship with User -->

        <one-to-one name="user"
class="com.example.entity.User"
constrained="true"/>

    </class>

</hibernate-mapping>
```

In this example, the primary key of the `profiles` table is the same as that of the `users` table, indicating that the profile is tightly coupled to a single user (one-to-one relationship).

Annotation-Based Mapping

Annotations are the most commonly used method in modern Hibernate applications for mapping Java classes to database tables. They are more concise and integrate the mapping configuration directly into the Java code, eliminating the need for separate XML files.

Example of Mapping a Class with Annotations

Let's revisit the `User` class, but this time using annotations:

```java
import javax.persistence.Entity;

import javax.persistence.Id;

import javax.persistence.GeneratedValue;

import javax.persistence.GenerationType;
```

```
import javax.persistence.Column;

@Entity
public class User {
    @Id
    @GeneratedValue(strategy =
GenerationType.IDENTITY)
    private Long id;

    @Column(name = "name", nullable = false)
    private String name;

    @Column(name = "email", nullable = false,
unique = true)
    private String email;

    // Getters and setters
}
```

Key Annotations

1. **@Entity**: Marks the class as an entity that will be mapped to a database table.

2. **@Id**: Specifies the primary key field.

3. **@GeneratedValue**: Defines how the primary key is generated. `GenerationType.IDENTITY` means that the database will handle ID generation.

4. **@Column**: Specifies the column name and constraints in the database (e.g., nullable, unique).

Example of One-to-One Relationship with Annotations

Suppose we have a one-to-one relationship between `User` and `Profile`. Here's how to map this relationship using annotations:

```java
import javax.persistence.Entity;
import javax.persistence.Id;
import javax.persistence.GeneratedValue;
import javax.persistence.GenerationType;
import javax.persistence.OneToOne;
import javax.persistence.CascadeType;

@Entity
public class User {
    @Id
    @GeneratedValue(strategy = GenerationType.IDENTITY)
    private Long id;

    private String name;
    private String email;
```

```
    @OneToOne(mappedBy = "user", cascade
= CascadeType.ALL)
    private Profile profile;

    // Getters and setters
}
```

```java
import javax.persistence.Entity;
import javax.persistence.Id;
import javax.persistence.GeneratedValue;
import javax.persistence.GenerationType;
import javax.persistence.OneToOne;

@Entity
public class Profile {
    @Id
```

```
    @GeneratedValue(strategy = GenerationType.IDENTITY)
    private Long id;

    private String biography;

    @OneToOne
    private User user;

    // Getters and setters
}
```

In this example:

- **@OneToOne**: Indicates a one-to-one relationship. The `mappedBy` attribute specifies that the relationship is bidirectional and managed by the `User` entity. The `cascade` attribute ensures that when a user is saved or deleted, their profile is also saved or deleted.

Association Types in Hibernate

Hibernate supports various types of associations between entities, reflecting relationships between database tables. These associations can be mapped using both annotations and XML.

One-to-One

A **One-to-One** relationship indicates that one entity is associated with exactly one instance of another entity. A classic example is the relationship between `User` and `Profile`, where each user has one profile, and each profile belongs to one user.

Example of One-to-One (Annotations)

As seen in the earlier example, a one-to-one relationship can be implemented using the `@OneToOne` annotation.

```java
@Entity
public class User {
    @Id
    @GeneratedValue(strategy = GenerationType.IDENTITY)
    private Long id;

    private String name;
    private String email;

    @OneToOne(mappedBy = "user", cascade = CascadeType.ALL)
    private Profile profile;
```

// Getters and setters

}

```

#### One-to-Many

A **One-to-Many** relationship means that one entity is associated with multiple instances of another entity. A common example is the relationship between a `User` and their `Orders`: a user can have multiple orders, but an order belongs to only one user.

##### Example of One-to-Many (Annotations)

```java

@Entity

public class User {

```java
    @Id
    @GeneratedValue(strategy = GenerationType.IDENTITY)
    private Long id;

    private String name;
    private String email;

    @OneToMany(mappedBy = "user", cascade = CascadeType.ALL)
    private Set<Order> orders = new HashSet<>();

    // Getters and setters
}
```

```java
@Entity
```

```java
public class Order {

    @Id

    @GeneratedValue(strategy = GenerationType.IDENTITY)

    private Long id;



    private String description;



    @ManyToOne

    @JoinColumn(name = "user_id")

    private User user;



    // Getters and setters

}
```

In this example:

- **@OneToMany**: Used in the `User` class to indicate that a user can have multiple orders.

- **@ManyToOne**: Used in the `Order` class to indicate that an order belongs to a single user.

Many-to-One

The **Many-to-One** relationship is the inverse of the One-to-Many relationship. This occurs when many instances of one entity are associated with one instance of another entity.

Example of Many-to-One (Annotations)

The Many-to-One relationship has already been illustrated in the previous example with the `Order` and `User` classes. Multiple orders can belong to a single user, and the mapping is managed with the `@ManyToOne` annotation.

Many-to-Many

A **Many-to-Many** relationship means that multiple instances of one entity are associated with multiple instances of another entity. A classic example is the relationship between `Student` and `Course`, where a student can enroll in multiple courses, and a course can have many students enrolled.

Example of Many-to-Many (Annotations)

```java
@Entity
public class Student {
    @Id
    @GeneratedValue(strategy = GenerationType.IDENTITY)
    private Long id;
```

```
    private String name;

    @ManyToMany(cascade = {CascadeType.PERSIST, CascadeType.MERGE})
    @JoinTable(
        name = "student_course",
        joinColumns = @JoinColumn(name = "student_id"),
        inverseJoinColumns = @JoinColumn(name = "course_id")
    )
    private Set<Course> courses = new HashSet<>();

    // Getters and setters
}
```

```java
@Entity
public class Course {
    @Id
    @GeneratedValue(strategy = GenerationType.IDENTITY)
    private Long id;

    private String title;

    @ManyToMany(mappedBy = "courses")
    private Set<Student> students = new HashSet<>();

    // Getters and setters
}
```

In this example:

- **@ManyToMany**: Indicates the many-to-many relationship between `Student` and `Course`.

- **@JoinTable**: Defines the join table that Hibernate will use to store the associations between students and courses.

Conclusion

Entity mapping in Hibernate is a fundamental aspect that effectively links Java classes to database tables. Through the use of annotations

and XML configurations, Hibernate enables seamless interactions with relational databases. Annotations are generally preferred in modern applications for their simplicity and integration with Java code, but XML still offers a clear, external configuration option that some projects may favor for certain use cases.

Additionally, understanding the different types of associations—such as **One-to-One**, **One-to-Many**, **Many-to-One**, and **Many-to-Many**—is essential for building well-structured data models that reflect the real-world relationships within a system. Hibernate provides powerful tools to manage these associations and automate many of the complexities involved in database operations.

Ultimately, the flexibility of Hibernate entity mapping allows developers to choose the approach that best suits their project's requirements while maintaining control over how data is managed and persisted.

4.Queries in Hibernate

One of the most powerful aspects of Hibernate is its ability to execute queries to retrieve, update, or delete data from the database. Hibernate offers several ways to interact with the database: from its proprietary language (HQL), to the Criteria API, and even native SQL queries. Each approach has its advantages and can be used in different scenarios, depending on the specific needs of the application.

In this guide, we will explore the following query methods in Hibernate:

- Hibernate Query Language (HQL)
- Criteria API
- Named Queries
- Native SQL Queries

Hibernate Query Language (HQL)

Hibernate Query Language (HQL) is an object-oriented query language that operates on Hibernate entities rather than directly on database tables. It is similar to SQL but works with Java classes and properties instead of database tables and columns. HQL allows you to write queries that are portable across different databases without needing to change the query syntax for each underlying database type.

Basic HQL Syntax

In HQL, mapped classes and their properties are used in queries instead of tables and columns. The HQL syntax includes:

- **SELECT**: Retrieves persistent objects

from the database.

- **FROM**: Specifies the entity (class) being queried.

- **WHERE**: Defines conditions to filter the results.

- **ORDER BY**: Sorts results based on one or more entity properties.

- **JOIN**: Joins multiple entities based on defined relationships.

Example of a Simple HQL Query

Suppose we have a `User` class and we want to retrieve all users from the database.

```java
String hql = "FROM User";

Query query = session.createQuery(hql);

List<User> results = query.list();
```

In this example:

- **`FROM User`**: This is an HQL query that retrieves all persisted `User` objects from the database. Note that we are using the class name `User`, not the database table name.

- **`session.createQuery(hql)`**: Creates a `Query` object that can be executed to fetch the results.

Query with `WHERE` Condition

If we want to filter users based on their email, we can add a `WHERE` clause:

```java
String hql = "FROM User WHERE email = :email";

Query query = session.createQuery(hql);
```

```
query.setParameter("email", "example@example.com");

List<User> results = query.list();
```

In this example:

- **`:email`**: This is a named parameter in the query, later replaced with the actual value using `setParameter`.

Select Specific Fields in a Query

HQL also allows selecting specific fields from an entity:

```java
String hql = "SELECT name, email FROM User";

Query query = session.createQuery(hql);
```

```
List<Object[]> results = query.list();
```

Here, we are selecting only the `name` and `email` fields from the `User` class. The result is a list of object arrays (`Object[]`), where each array contains the values of the selected fields.

Join in HQL

HQL supports join operations to navigate between related entities. Suppose we have a `One-to-Many` relationship between `User` and `Order`, where a user can have many orders.

```java
String hql = "FROM User u JOIN u.orders o WHERE u.id = :userId";

Query query = session.createQuery(hql);
```

query.setParameter("userId", 1L);

List<Object[]> results = query.list();

```

In this example:

- **`JOIN`**: Joins the `User` and `Order` entities based on the relationship defined in the Java entities. The `orders` property is a collection of orders associated with the user.

- **`u.id = :userId`**: This is the condition filtering users by their ID.

#### Update Query in HQL

In addition to retrieving data, HQL allows you to perform update or delete operations. For example, to update a user's email:

```java

```
String hql = "UPDATE User SET email = :newEmail WHERE id = :userId";

Query query = session.createQuery(hql);

query.setParameter("newEmail", "new@example.com");

query.setParameter("userId", 1L);

int result = query.executeUpdate();
```

In this example:

- **`UPDATE`**: Specifies that we are updating the `User` entity.

- **`executeUpdate()`**: Executes the query and returns the number of rows affected.

Delete Query in HQL

To delete a user from the database:

```java
String hql = "DELETE FROM User WHERE id = :userId";

Query query = session.createQuery(hql);

query.setParameter("userId", 1L);

int result = query.executeUpdate();
```

This query deletes the user with ID `1` from the table.

Criteria API

Hibernate's **Criteria API** provides a programmatic way to build dynamic queries. Unlike HQL, where queries are expressed in a string, the Criteria API uses an object-oriented approach to construct queries. This approach is useful when you need to build queries dynamically or want to take advantage of code auto-completion provided by IDEs.

Building a Query with Criteria API

To build a query using the Criteria API, you start with the Hibernate session, create an instance of `Criteria`, and add query conditions using methods.

Example of a Simple Query with Criteria API

Suppose we want to retrieve all users from the database:

```java
CriteriaBuilder builder =
session.getCriteriaBuilder();
```

```
CriteriaQuery<User> criteria =
builder.createQuery(User.class);

Root<User> root = criteria.from(User.class);

criteria.select(root);

Query<User> query =
session.createQuery(criteria);

List<User> results = query.getResultList();
```

In this example:

- **`CriteriaBuilder`**: This is the entry point for creating queries with the Criteria API.

- **`CriteriaQuery<User>`**: Defines a query to retrieve `User` entities.

- **`Root<User>`**: Represents the root entity of the query (`User` in this case).

- **`session.createQuery(criteria)`**: Creates a Hibernate query from the Criteria API query.

Query with `WHERE` Condition Using Criteria API

To add conditions to the query, use the `where` method:

```java
CriteriaBuilder builder = session.getCriteriaBuilder();
CriteriaQuery<User> criteria = builder.createQuery(User.class);
Root<User> root = criteria.from(User.class);
criteria.select(root).where(builder.equal(root.get("email"), "example@example.com"));
Query<User> query = session.createQuery(criteria);
List<User> results = query.getResultList();
```

In this example:

- **`builder.equal(root.get("email"), "example@example.com")`**: Creates a `WHERE` condition to filter users based on their email.

Query with Sorting

To sort the results, use the `orderBy` method:

```java
CriteriaBuilder builder = session.getCriteriaBuilder();

CriteriaQuery<User> criteria = builder.createQuery(User.class);

Root<User> root = criteria.from(User.class);

criteria.select(root).orderBy(builder.asc(root.get("name")));

Query<User> query =
```

```
session.createQuery(criteria);

List<User> results = query.getResultList();
```

Here, we are sorting the results by the `name` field in ascending order.

Join in Criteria API

Just like HQL, we can perform joins between related entities:

```java
CriteriaBuilder builder =
session.getCriteriaBuilder();

CriteriaQuery<Object[]> criteria =
builder.createQuery(Object[].class);

Root<User> root = criteria.from(User.class);

Join<User, Order> ordersJoin =
root.join("orders");
```

```
criteria.multiselect(root.get("name"), ordersJoin.get("description"));

Query<Object[]> query = session.createQuery(criteria);

List<Object[]> results = query.getResultList();
```

In this example:

- **`root.join("orders")`**: Joins the `User` entity with the associated `orders` collection.

- **`criteria.multiselect`**: Selects multiple fields from the joined entities.

Named Queries

Named Queries in Hibernate are

predefined queries that are specified in entity annotations or mapping files. They are defined with a name and can be used throughout the application without rewriting the same query each time.

Defining a Named Query with Annotations

Here is how to define a `NamedQuery` using annotations:

```java
@Entity
@NamedQueries({
    @NamedQuery(name = "findUserByEmail", query = "FROM User WHERE email = :email")
})
public class User {
    // Class definition
```

}

```

In this example:

- **`@NamedQuery`**: Defines a named query called `findUserByEmail` that retrieves the user based on their email.

### Using a Named Query

Once defined, a named query can be used as follows:

```java
Query query =
session.getNamedQuery("findUserByEmail");
query.setParameter("email",
"example@example.com");
List<User> results = query.list();
```
```

```

This code retrieves the user with the email "example@example.com" using the `findUserByEmail` named query.

### Named Native Queries

**Named Native Queries** are similar to `NamedQueries` but use native SQL instead of HQL. Here's an example of defining one:

```java
@Entity
@NamedNativeQuery(
    name = "findAllUsersSQL",
    query = "SELECT * FROM users",
    resultClass = User.class
)

```
public class User {
    // Class definition
}
```

This native SQL query can be executed the same way as named HQL queries:

```java
Query query = session.getNamedQuery("findAllUsersSQL");
List<User> results = query.list();
```

Native SQL Queries

Hibernate also allows the execution of

Native SQL Queries, which are queries written directly in SQL.

This is useful when you want to leverage database-specific features or write highly optimized SQL queries.

Executing a Native SQL Query

Here's how to execute a native SQL query:

```java
String sql = "SELECT * FROM users";
SQLQuery query = session.createSQLQuery(sql);
query.addEntity(User.class);
List<User> results = query.list();
```

In this example:

- **`session.createSQLQuery(sql)`**: Creates a native SQL query.

- **`query.addEntity(User.class)`**: Maps the result set to the `User` entity class.

Native SQL with Parameters

Native SQL queries can also accept parameters:

```java
String sql = "SELECT * FROM users WHERE email = :email";

SQLQuery query = session.createSQLQuery(sql);

query.setParameter("email", "example@example.com");

query.addEntity(User.class);
```

```
List<User> results = query.list();
```

Here, the `:email` parameter is bound to the actual value "example@example.com" using `setParameter`.

Hibernate offers a variety of ways to perform queries, including HQL, the Criteria API, Named Queries, and Native SQL queries. Each of these approaches provides a different level of flexibility and control. HQL is great for simple, portable queries; the Criteria API is ideal for dynamic, programmatic queries; Named Queries provide a reusable query solution; and Native SQL is useful for database-specific optimizations.

5.CRUD Operations in Hibernate

CRUD operations (Create, Read, Update, Delete) represent the fundamental actions for managing data in any database-driven application. Hibernate, as an ORM (Object-Relational Mapping) framework, simplifies the implementation of these operations by mapping Java entities to database tables and handling data persistence.

In this article, we will explore CRUD operations in Hibernate in detail, using practical examples to demonstrate how to perform each one:

- Persisting an Object (Create)

- Retrieving an Object (Read)

- Updating an Object (Update)

- Deleting an Object (Delete)

---

1. Persisting an Object (Create)

Persistence of an object refers to the process of saving a Java object to the database. Hibernate translates the object into a database row, inserting its data into the corresponding columns.

Steps for Object Persistence

1. **Create a Session**: The Hibernate session is the starting point for all CRUD operations. A session is obtained from the `SessionFactory`.

2. **Begin a Transaction**: Write operations must be performed within a transaction to ensure data integrity.

3. **Use the `save` Method**: The session's `save` method is used to save a new object to the database.

4. **Commit the Transaction**: After saving the object, the transaction must be committed to make the operation permanent in the database.

Example of Object Persistence

Suppose we have a class `User` mapped to a `users` table:

```java
@Entity
@Table(name = "users")
public class User {
    @Id
    @GeneratedValue(strategy = GenerationType.IDENTITY)
    private Long id;

    private String name;
```

```
    private String email;

    // Getters and setters
}
```

To save a new user to the database:

```java
// Creating the session
Session session = HibernateUtil.getSessionFactory().openSession();
Transaction transaction = null;

try {
    // Begin the transaction
    transaction = session.beginTransaction();
```

```
        // Creating a new User object
        User user = new User();
        user.setName("John Doe");
        user.setEmail("john.doe@example.com");

        // Saving the object to the database
        session.save(user);

        // Commit the transaction
        transaction.commit();
    } catch (Exception e) {
        if (transaction != null) {
            transaction.rollback();
        }
        e.printStackTrace();
    } finally {
        session.close();
    }
```

```

### Process Details

- **`session.save(user)`**: This method is responsible for persisting the `user` object in the database. Hibernate generates an SQL `INSERT INTO` query to insert the values of the `user` object into the `users` table.

- **`transaction.commit()`**: The transaction must be committed to confirm the operation. If not committed, the changes won't be saved to the database.

- **Exception Handling**: In case of an error, the transaction is rolled back to undo any partial changes.

---

## 2. Retrieving an Object (Read)
```

Fetching data from the database is one of the primary operations in any application. Hibernate provides several ways to retrieve objects, such as using the `get` or `load` method, HQL (Hibernate Query Language), Criteria API, and native SQL queries.

Retrieving an Object Using the `get` Method

The **`get`** method is used to retrieve a single object from the database based on its identifier (primary key). If the object does not exist, the method returns `null`.

Example of Retrieving with `get`

To retrieve a `User` object with a specific ID:

```java
// Creating the session
```

```
Session session =
HibernateUtil.getSessionFactory().openSessio
n();


try {

   // Retrieving the User object with ID 1

   User user = session.get(User.class, 1L);



   if (user != null) {

       System.out.println("Name: " +
user.getName());

       System.out.println("Email: " +
user.getEmail());

    } else {

       System.out.println("User not found");

    }

 } catch (Exception e) {

    e.printStackTrace();

 } finally {
```

    session.close();
}
```

In this example:

- **`session.get(User.class, 1L)`**: Retrieves the user with ID `1` from the database. If the user does not exist, the method returns `null`.

### Difference Between `get` and `load`

- **`get`**: Immediately fetches the object from the database. If the object does not exist, it returns `null`.

- **`load`**: Returns a proxy (a placeholder object) and fetches the actual object when it is accessed (lazy loading). If the object does not exist, it throws an `ObjectNotFoundException`.
```

Example with `load`

```java
User user = session.load(User.class, 1L);
System.out.println("Name: " + user.getName());  // Accessing 'getName()' forces the load
```

With `load`, the object is retrieved only when it is actually used (e.g., when accessing the `name` property).

Retrieving with HQL

In addition to `get` and `load`, we can use HQL to execute more complex queries. Suppose we want to retrieve all users from the database:

```java
String hql = "FROM User";
Query query = session.createQuery(hql);
List<User> users = query.list();

for (User user : users) {
    System.out.println(user.getName() + " - " + user.getEmail());
}
```

In this case:

- **`FROM User`**: This is an HQL query that retrieves all `User` objects from the database.

- **`query.list()`**: Returns a list of `User` objects.

---

3. Updating an Object (Update)

Updating an object involves modifying one or more fields of an existing object and synchronizing these changes with the database. Hibernate provides several methods for updating objects, including `update`, `merge`, and automatic operations when an object is in a persistent state.

Updating an Object Using the `update` Method

The **`update`** method is used to synchronize a transient or detached object with the database, updating its fields.

Example of Updating with `update`

Suppose we want to update the email of a user:

```java
// Creating the session
Session session =
HibernateUtil.getSessionFactory().openSessio
n();
Transaction transaction = null;

try {
    // Begin the transaction
    transaction = session.beginTransaction();

    // Retrieve the user
    User user = session.get(User.class, 1L);

    if (user != null) {
        // Update the email
```

```
user.setEmail("new.email@example.com");

      // Update the object in the database
      session.update(user);
    }

    // Commit the transaction
    transaction.commit();
} catch (Exception e) {
    if (transaction != null) {
        transaction.rollback();
    }
    e.printStackTrace();
} finally {
    session.close();
}
```

In this example:

- **`session.update(user)`**: Updates the `user` object in the database with the new values (in this case, the email).

Difference Between `update` and `merge`

- **`update`**: Updates the object in the database but may throw an exception if the object is already associated with a different session.

- **`merge`**: Copies the state of an object into one managed by the current session. It can be used to avoid session management issues.

Example with `merge`

```java
```

```
User user = new User();
user.setId(1L);
user.setEmail("new.email@example.com");

session.merge(user);
```

In this example, even though the `user` object is not managed by the session, `merge` will update the corresponding data in the database.

---

4. Deleting an Object (Delete)

Deleting an object in Hibernate allows you to remove a persisted entity from the database. When you delete an object, Hibernate handles the operation through transactions, ensuring that the action is executed safely and consistently.

Example of Deleting an Object in Hibernate

Let’s assume we have an entity called `Student` with a simple configuration:

```java
@Entity
@Table(name = "students")
public class Student {
    @Id
    @GeneratedValue(strategy = GenerationType.IDENTITY)
    private Long id;

    private String firstName;
    private String lastName;
```

// Getters and Setters

}

```

### Steps to Delete an Object in Hibernate

#### a. Create a Session

You need to begin a transaction and obtain a session from Hibernate.

```java

SessionFactory sessionFactory = HibernateUtil.getSessionFactory();

Session session = sessionFactory.openSession();

Transaction transaction = null;

```
try {
    transaction = session.beginTransaction();

    // Step 2: Retrieve the object to be deleted
    Long studentId = 1L; // ID of the student to
be deleted
    Student student = session.get(Student.class,
studentId);

    if (student != null) {
        // Step 3: Delete the object
        session.delete(student);
        System.out.println("Student with ID: " +
studentId + " has been deleted.");
    } else {
        System.out.println("Student with ID: " +
studentId + " not found.");
    }
```

```
    // Step 4: Commit the transaction
    transaction.commit();
} catch (Exception e) {
    if (transaction != null) {
        transaction.rollback();
    }
    e.printStackTrace();
} finally {
    session.close();
}
```

Code Explanation

1. **Session and Transaction Creation**: A new session is opened, and a transaction is initiated.

Code Explanation (continued)

2. **Retrieve the Object**: Using `session.get()`, the `Student` object with a specific ID is retrieved.

3. **Delete the Object**: If the object is found, the `session.delete()` method is invoked to remove the object from the persistence context.

4. **Commit the Transaction**: If everything goes well, the transaction is committed to make the changes persistent in the database.

5. **Error Handling**: In case of an error, a rollback is performed to undo the transaction.

6. **Close the Session**: Finally, the session is closed to free up resources.

Final Considerations

Deleting an object involves removing it from the database, but be cautious about referential integrity constraints: if there are other entities referencing the `Student` object, Hibernate may throw an exception if you attempt to delete an associated object. To manage this situation, you may need to implement logic to delete associated entities first or define deletion policies on the database constraints.

Summary

This guide has provided an overview of CRUD operations in Hibernate, highlighting how to create, read, update, and delete entities. By leveraging Hibernate's capabilities, developers can efficiently manage data persistence while ensuring data integrity and consistency in their applications. Whether you are working on a small project or a large-scale application, understanding these CRUD operations is essential for effective database management.

6. Transaction Management in Hibernate

Hibernate is a powerful ORM (Object-Relational Mapping) framework that simplifies transaction management in Java projects. Proper transaction management is essential to ensure data consistency and integrity in the database. In this article, we will explore:

- **Transactions in Hibernate**
- **Transaction Management**
- **Transaction Isolation Levels**

Additionally, we will cover **fetching strategies** and **performance management techniques**, including:

- **Eager vs Lazy Loading**
- **Strategies to Optimize Fetching**
- **Query Optimization**

- **Caching in Hibernate (First-Level and Second-Level Cache)**

- **Performance Profiling**

Transactions in Hibernate

A **transaction** is a sequence of operations that are executed as a single unit of work. In a database context, a transaction ensures that all operations are completed successfully or, in case of an error, that no changes are made to the database.

Transaction Properties

Transactions must satisfy the ACID properties:

1. **Atomicity**: All operations within a transaction must be completed; if one fails, all others must be rolled back.

2. **Consistency**: The transaction must bring the database from one valid state to another valid state.

3. **Isolation**: Transactions must be executed in isolation from one another.

4. **Durability**: Once a transaction is committed, the changes must be permanent even in case of system failures.

Transactions in Hibernate

Hibernate manages transactions through the `Transaction` class, which represents an ongoing transaction. You can create and manage transactions using the following workflow:

1. Open a session.

2. Start a transaction.

3. Perform operations (save, update, delete).

4. Commit the transaction or roll back in case

of an error.

Example of a Transaction

```java
Session session = HibernateUtil.getSessionFactory().openSession();
Transaction transaction = null;

try {
    transaction = session.beginTransaction();

    // Persistence operations
    User user = new User();
    user.setName("Giovanni");
    user.setEmail("giovanni@example.com");
    session.save(user);
```

```
    // Commit the transaction
    transaction.commit();
} catch (Exception e) {
    if (transaction != null) {
        transaction.rollback();
    }
    e.printStackTrace();
} finally {
    session.close();
}
```

In this example:

- The transaction begins with `transaction = session.beginTransaction()`.
- If all operations complete successfully, `transaction.commit()` is called to make the changes permanent in the database.

- In case of an error, the `catch` block rolls back the transaction to undo partial changes.

Transaction Management

Transaction management in Hibernate can vary depending on the application context. There are various ways to manage transactions, depending on how you want them to be configured.

Programmatic Transaction Management

Programmatic transaction management involves using the `Transaction` class and session methods such as `beginTransaction`, `commit`, and `rollback`, as shown in the previous example. This approach offers detailed control over transaction management.

Transaction Management with Spring

If you are using Spring with Hibernate, you can simplify transaction management using Spring's transaction support. With Spring, you can use the `@Transactional` annotation to automatically manage transactions:

```java
@Service
public class UserService {

    @Transactional
    public void createUser(User user) {
        session.save(user);
    }
}
```

In this example, Spring automatically handles the beginning and committing of the transaction. If an exception occurs within the method, Spring will automatically roll back the transaction.

Transaction Isolation Levels

The **isolation level** determines how and when changes made by a transaction are visible to other transactions. There are four standard isolation levels defined by the SQL standard:

1. **Read Uncommitted**: Allows a transaction to read data modified by other transactions, even if those have not yet been committed. This level is the least secure and can lead to dirty reads.

2. **Read Committed**: Allows a transaction to read only data that has been committed by other transactions. This level avoids dirty reads but can still lead to non-repeatable reads.

3. **Repeatable Read**: Ensures that if a transaction reads data, it will not change during the transaction's duration. This level prevents dirty reads and non-repeatable reads but does not prevent phantom reads.

4. **Serializable**: This is the strictest isolation level. Each transaction is executed as if it were the only transaction in the system. This level prevents dirty reads, non-repeatable reads, and phantom reads but has a significant performance cost.

Setting the Isolation Level

In Hibernate, you can set the isolation level for a transaction using the `setTransactionIsolation` method of the session or by configuring properties in the Hibernate configuration file.

```java
```

```
session.doWork(connection -> {

connection.setTransactionIsolation(Connection.TRANSACTION_SERIALIZABLE);
});
```

Fetching Strategies in Hibernate

The **fetching** strategy refers to how Hibernate retrieves data associated with objects. There are two main approaches for fetching data: **Eager Loading** and **Lazy Loading**.

Eager vs Lazy Loading

1. **Eager Loading**: With this strategy, Hibernate immediately loads all data associated with an object as soon as the object itself is loaded. This is useful when you know

in advance that the associated data will be needed.

Example:

```java
@Entity
public class User {
    @OneToMany(fetch =
FetchType.EAGER)
    private List<Order> orders;

    // Other fields and methods
}
```

In this example, all orders associated with a user will be loaded immediately when the `User` object is retrieved.

2. **Lazy Loading**: With this strategy, associated data is loaded only when it is actually needed. This can improve performance by reducing the initial load, but it requires that the Hibernate session remain open until the data is accessed.

Example:

```java
@Entity
public class User {
    @OneToMany(fetch = FetchType.LAZY)
    private List<Order> orders;

    // Other fields and methods
}
```

In this case, the associated orders will not be loaded until the `orders` property is accessed.

Strategies to Optimize Fetching

To optimize data fetching in Hibernate, consider the following strategies:

- **Using JOIN FETCH**: In HQL, you can use `JOIN FETCH` to load associated entities in a single query.

```java
String hql = "SELECT u FROM User u JOIN FETCH u.orders";
List<User> users = session.createQuery(hql, User.class).getResultList();
```

- **Batch Fetching**: Configure batch

fetching to load associations in chunks, reducing the number of queries executed.

```java
@BatchSize(size = 10)
@OneToMany(fetch = FetchType.LAZY)
private List<Order> orders;
```

- **Using Second-Level Cache**: Second-level caching can reduce the number of database accesses, improving performance in applications with high read traffic.

Performance Management

Performance management is crucial for applications using Hibernate, as inefficient configuration can lead to significant slowdowns. Here are some techniques to improve performance.

Query Optimization

Hibernate queries can be optimized in various ways:

- **Using HQL**: HQL queries are more efficient than SQL queries because they operate at a higher level, allowing Hibernate to generate more optimal SQL.

- **Using Projections**: If you only need some fields, use projections to retrieve only the necessary data.

```java
String hql = "SELECT u.name, u.email FROM User u";
List<Object[]> results = session.createQuery(hql).getResultList();
```

- **Indexing**: Ensure that the most frequently used columns in queries are indexed in the database to improve data access performance.

Caching in Hibernate

Caching is a fundamental mechanism for improving the performance of Hibernate applications. There are two levels of cache:

1. **First-Level Cache**: Each Hibernate session has its own first-level cache, which stores loaded objects. If an object has already been loaded in the current session, Hibernate will return the object from the cache rather than executing a query to the database.

2. **Second-Level Cache**: This cache is shared among all sessions and can be used to store objects that do not change frequently. The second-level cache can be configured to

use different caching providers, such as Ehcache or Infinispan.

Configuring Second-Level Cache

To enable the second-level cache, you need to configure it in the `hibernate.cfg.xml` file:

```xml
<property name="hibernate.cache.use_second_level_cache">true</property>
<property name="hibernate.cache.region.factory_class">org.hibernate.cache.ehcache.EhCacheRegionFactory</property>
```

Additionally, you can enable caching for specific entities using the `@Cache` annotation:

```java
@Entity
@Cacheable
@Cache(usage = CacheConcurrencyStrategy.READ_WRITE)
public class User {
    // Fields and methods
}
```

Performance Profiling

To identify performance bottlenecks in Hibernate applications, you can use profiling tools such as:

- **Hibernate Statistics**: Hibernate provides a `Statistics` class that allows you to gather data on query performance and loading operations.

```java
Statistics stats =
sessionFactory.getStatistics();
stats.setStatisticsEnabled(true);
// Execute some operations
System.out.println("Query executed: " +
stats.getQueryExecutionCount());
```

- **Database Monitoring Tools**: Use tools like JMX (Java Management Extensions) or database profiling tools to monitor executed SQL queries and execution time.

Transaction management, fetching strategies, and performance management are fundamental aspects in the design of applications using Hibernate. Understanding how to properly manage transactions ensures data consistency, while optimizing queries and using caching can significantly improve application performance.

By implementing the best practices described above, you can develop robust, scalable, and performant Hibernate applications.

7.Integration with Hibernate Framework and Technologies

Hibernate is one of the most popular ORM (Object-Relational Mapping) frameworks in the Java world. It is widely used to simplify data persistence in enterprise applications, thanks to its ability to abstract the complexities of database interactions. In this article, we will explore the various ways to integrate Hibernate with other frameworks and technologies, including:

- **Hibernate with Spring**
- **Hibernate with JPA**
- **Hibernate and RESTful Services**

Subsequently, we will discuss **best practices** and **error handling**, covering:

- **Best practices for using Hibernate**

- **Exception handling**

- **Logging strategy**

Hibernate with Spring

Introduction to Spring

Spring is a powerful framework for Java application development, offering a vast ecosystem of tools and modules to simplify building scalable and maintainable applications. One of the most commonly used modules is **Spring Data**, which provides an abstraction for database interaction, making it easier to integrate with various ORMs, including Hibernate.

Configuring Hibernate with Spring

To integrate Hibernate with Spring, you can use either XML-based or annotation-based configuration. Here, we'll focus on annotation-based configuration, which is the most common and modern approach.

1. **Add Maven dependencies**: Ensure that you have the following dependencies in your `pom.xml` file:

```xml
<dependency>

<groupId>org.springframework</groupId>
    <artifactId>spring-context</artifactId>
    <version>5.3.13</version>
</dependency>
<dependency>

<groupId>org.springframework</groupId>
    <artifactId>spring-orm</artifactId>
    <version>5.3.13</version>
```

```
</dependency>
<dependency>
    <groupId>org.hibernate</groupId>
    <artifactId>hibernate-core</artifactId>
    <version>5.6.3.Final</version>
</dependency>
<dependency>
    <groupId>org.hibernate</groupId>
    <artifactId>hibernate-
entitymanager</artifactId>
    <version>5.6.3.Final</version>
</dependency>
<dependency>
    <groupId>javax.transaction</groupId>
    <artifactId>jta</artifactId>
    <version>1.2</version>
</dependency>
<dependency>
```

```
    <groupId>mysql</groupId>
    <artifactId>mysql-connector-java</artifactId>
    <version>8.0.25</version>
  </dependency>
```

2. **Configure the DataSource**: You can configure the DataSource using Spring annotations.

```java
import org.springframework.context.annotation.Bean;
import org.springframework.context.annotation.Configuration;
import org.springframework.jdbc.datasource.DriverManagerDataSource;
```

```
import javax.sql.DataSource;

@Configuration
public class DataSourceConfig {
    @Bean
    public DataSource dataSource() {
        DriverManagerDataSource dataSource = new DriverManagerDataSource();
        dataSource.setDriverClassName("com.mysql.cj.jdbc.Driver");
        dataSource.setUrl("jdbc:mysql://localhost:3306/your_database");
        dataSource.setUsername("your_username");
        dataSource.setPassword("your_password");
        return dataSource;
    }
```

}
```

3. **Configure Hibernate**: You can configure Hibernate using `LocalSessionFactoryBean`.

```java
import org.hibernate.SessionFactory;

import
org.springframework.beans.factory.annotation
.Autowired;

import
org.springframework.context.annotation.Bean;

import
org.springframework.context.annotation.Confi
guration;

import
org.springframework.orm.hibernate5.LocalSes
sionFactoryBean;

import
```
```

```
org.springframework.orm.hibernate5.Hibernat
eTransactionManager;

  import
org.springframework.transaction.annotation.E
nableTransactionManagement;


  import javax.sql.DataSource;

  import java.util.Properties;


  @Configuration

  @EnableTransactionManagement

  public class HibernateConfig {


      @Autowired

      private DataSource dataSource;


      @Bean

      public LocalSessionFactoryBean
sessionFactory() {
```

```
        LocalSessionFactoryBean
sessionFactory = new
LocalSessionFactoryBean();

sessionFactory.setDataSource(dataSource);

sessionFactory.setPackagesToScan("com.exa
mple.your_package"); // Change to your
package

sessionFactory.setHibernateProperties(hiberna
teProperties());

        return sessionFactory;

    }


    @Bean

    public HibernateTransactionManager
transactionManager(SessionFactory
sessionFactory) {

        HibernateTransactionManager
txManager = new
HibernateTransactionManager();
```

```
txManager.setSessionFactory(sessionFactory);
        return txManager;
    }

    private Properties hibernateProperties() {
        Properties properties = new
Properties();
        properties.put("hibernate.dialect",
"org.hibernate.dialect.MySQL5Dialect");
        properties.put("hibernate.show_sql",
"true");

properties.put("hibernate.hbm2ddl.auto",
"update");
        return properties;
    }
}
```

Using Hibernate in a Spring Service

Now that Hibernate is configured with Spring, you can start using persistence features. For example, you can create a service to handle CRUD operations:

```java
import org.springframework.beans.factory.annotation.Autowired;

import org.springframework.stereotype.Service;

import org.springframework.transaction.annotation.Transactional;


import java.util.List;


@Service

public class UserService {
```

```
@Autowired
private SessionFactory sessionFactory;

@Transactional
public void saveUser(User user) {

sessionFactory.getCurrentSession().save(user)
;
}

@Transactional(readOnly = true)
public User findUser(Long id) {
    return
sessionFactory.getCurrentSession().get(User.c
lass, id);
}

@Transactional
```

```
    public void updateUser(User user) {

sessionFactory.getCurrentSession().update(us
er);
    }

    @Transactional
    public void deleteUser(Long id) {
        User user = findUser(id);
        if (user != null) {

sessionFactory.getCurrentSession().delete(use
r);
        }
    }

    @Transactional(readOnly = true)
    public List<User> findAllUsers() {
        return
sessionFactory.getCurrentSession().createQue
```

```
ry("FROM User", User.class).list();
    }
}
```

In this example, `UserService` uses Hibernate to handle CRUD operations. The `@Transactional` annotations automatically manage transactions.

Hibernate with JPA

Introduction to JPA

The Java Persistence API (JPA) is a standard interface for data persistence in Java. Hibernate is one of the most widely used JPA implementations and allows you to use JPA annotations to define entities and relationships.

Configuring Hibernate with JPA

To configure Hibernate with JPA, follow these steps:

1. **Add Maven dependencies**: Ensure you have the JPA dependencies in your `pom.xml` file.

```xml
<dependency>
    <groupId>javax.persistence</groupId>
    <artifactId>javax.persistence-api</artifactId>
    <version>2.2</version>
</dependency>
```

2. **Create the configuration file**: Create a `persistence.xml` file in the `META-INF`

folder of your project.

```xml
<persistence
xmlns="http://xmlns.jcp.org/xml/ns/persistence"

xmlns:xsi="http://www.w3.org/2001/XMLSchema-instance"

xsi:schemaLocation="http://xmlns.jcp.org/xml/ns/persistence

http://xmlns.jcp.org/xml/ns/persistence/persistence_2_2.xsd"
             version="2.2">
    <persistence-unit
name="your_persistence_unit">

<provider>org.hibernate.jpa.HibernatePersistenceProvider</provider>
```

```
<class>com.example.your_package.User</cla
ss>

        <properties>

            <property
name="javax.persistence.jdbc.driver"
value="com.mysql.cj.jdbc.Driver"/>

            <property
name="javax.persistence.jdbc.url"
value="jdbc:mysql://localhost:3306/your_data
base"/>

            <property
name="javax.persistence.jdbc.user"
value="your_username"/>

            <property
name="javax.persistence.jdbc.password"
value="your_password"/>

            <property name="hibernate.dialect"
value="org.hibernate.dialect.MySQL5Dialect"
/>

            <property
name="hibernate.hbm2ddl.auto"
value="update"/>

        </properties>
```

```
    </persistence-unit>
</persistence>
```

Using JPA with Hibernate

You can use JPA with Hibernate to manage persistence. Here is an example of using `EntityManager` to handle entities:

```java
import javax.persistence.EntityManager;
import javax.persistence.EntityManagerFactory;
import javax.persistence.Persistence;
import java.util.List;

public class UserServiceJPA {
```

```
    private EntityManagerFactory emf =
Persistence.createEntityManagerFactory("you
r_persistence_unit");


    public void saveUser(User user) {
        EntityManager em =
emf.createEntityManager();
        em.getTransaction().begin();
        em.persist(user);
        em.getTransaction().commit();
        em.close();
    }


    public User findUser(Long id) {
        EntityManager em =
emf.createEntityManager();
        User user = em.find(User.class, id);
        em.close();
        return user;
```

```
}

public void updateUser(User user) {
    EntityManager em =
emf.createEntityManager();
    em.getTransaction().begin();
    em.merge(user);
    em.getTransaction().commit();
    em.close();
}

public void deleteUser(Long id) {
    EntityManager em =
emf.createEntityManager();
    em.getTransaction().begin();
    User user = em.find(User.class, id);
    if (user != null) {
        em.remove(user);
    }
```

```
        em.getTransaction().commit();
        em.close();
    }

    public List<User> findAllUsers() {
        EntityManager em =
emf.createEntityManager();
        List<User> users =
em.createQuery("FROM User",
User.class).getResultList();
        em.close();
        return users;
    }
}
```

In this example, `UserServiceJPA` uses `EntityManager` to handle entities.

Hibernate and RESTful Services

Integrating Hibernate with RESTful services is a common pattern in modern web applications. You can create a RESTful API to expose data persisted by Hibernate.

1. **Create a REST Controller**: Here's an example using Spring MVC to create a REST API.

```java
import org.springframework.beans.factory.annotation.Autowired;

import org.springframework.http.ResponseEntity;

import org.springframework.web.bind.annotation.*;
```

```
import java.util.List;

@RestController
@RequestMapping("/users")
public class UserController {

    @Autowired
    private UserService userService;

    @GetMapping
    public List<User> getAllUsers() {
        return userService.findAllUsers();
    }

    @GetMapping("/{id}")
    public ResponseEntity<User>
getUserById(@PathVariable Long id) {
```

```
        User user = userService.findUser(id);
        if (user == null) {
            return
ResponseEntity.notFound().build();
        }
        return ResponseEntity.ok(user);
    }

    @PostMapping
    public ResponseEntity<User>
createUser(@RequestBody User user) {
        userService.saveUser(user);
        return ResponseEntity.ok(user);
    }

    @PutMapping("/{id}")
    public ResponseEntity<User>
updateUser(@PathVariable Long id,
@RequestBody User updatedUser) {
```

```
        User user = userService.findUser(id);
        if (user == null) {
            return
ResponseEntity.notFound().build();
        }
        user.setName(updatedUser.getName());
        user.setEmail(updatedUser.getEmail());
        userService.updateUser(user);
        return ResponseEntity.ok(user);
    }

    @DeleteMapping("/{id}")
    public ResponseEntity<Void>
deleteUser(@PathVariable Long id) {
        userService.deleteUser(id);
        return ResponseEntity.ok().build();
    }
}
```

This API handles CRUD operations for users, leveraging Hibernate's data persistence capabilities.

Conclusion

Hibernate provides a flexible and powerful ORM solution for Java applications. By integrating it with frameworks like Spring and JPA, you can build scalable applications while reducing the complexity of database interaction. Furthermore, by exposing data through RESTful services, you can develop modern web applications that are easy to maintain and extend.

Best Practices for Using Hibernate

When using Hibernate, it’s important to follow some best practices to ensure performance, maintainability, and scalability:

1. **Use Lazy Loading**: By default, Hibernate loads relationships lazily, which means that related entities are not fetched until they are explicitly accessed. This improves performance by reducing unnecessary database queries.

2. **Use Batching for Bulk Operations**: When dealing with large data sets, use batch processing to improve performance.

```java
session.setJdbcBatchSize(50);
```

3. **Optimize HQL Queries**: Use efficient HQL (Hibernate Query Language) queries to minimize database load and fetch only the necessary data.

4. **Use Cache**: Hibernate provides first-level and second-level caching. First-level caching is enabled by default and is tied to the session scope. Second-level caching can be enabled for improved performance in long-running applications.

```java
@Cacheable
public class User {
    // ...
}
```

5. **Close Sessions Properly**: Always close Hibernate sessions properly to prevent memory leaks.

Exception Handling in Hibernate

Handling exceptions is crucial in Hibernate-based applications. Here's an example of handling Hibernate exceptions:

```java
try {
    session.beginTransaction();
    session.save(entity);
    session.getTransaction().commit();
} catch (HibernateException e) {
    if (session.getTransaction() != null) {
        session.getTransaction().rollback();
    }
    e.printStackTrace();
} finally {
    session.close();
}
```

Logging Strategy

To enable logging in Hibernate, configure `log4j` or `slf4j` to display SQL queries and other useful information. For example, you can enable SQL logging by adding the following properties:

```xml
<property name="hibernate.show_sql" value="true"/>
<property name="hibernate.format_sql" value="true"/>
```

This helps in monitoring SQL queries and understanding Hibernate's interaction with the database.

8.Practical Examples of Hibernate

In this section, we will explore a sample project that uses Hibernate as an ORM (Object-Relational Mapping) for data persistence management. We will focus on how to configure Hibernate, create entities, manage CRUD operations, and provide a RESTful interface for system interaction. Through practical code examples, we will demonstrate how to use Hibernate in real-world scenarios.

Sample Project with Hibernate

Project Description

Imagine you need to develop an application to manage users in a system. This application allows you to register, update, delete, and view users. We will use Hibernate to handle data persistence in a relational database (such as MySQL).

Project Structure

The project structure will be as follows:

```
hibernate-example/
│
├── src/
│   ├── main/
│   │   ├── java/
│   │   │   └── com/
│   │   │       └── example/
│   │   │           ├── config/
│   │   │           │   └── HibernateUtil.java
│   │   │           ├── entity/
│   │   │           │   └── User.java
│   │   │           ├── repository/
```

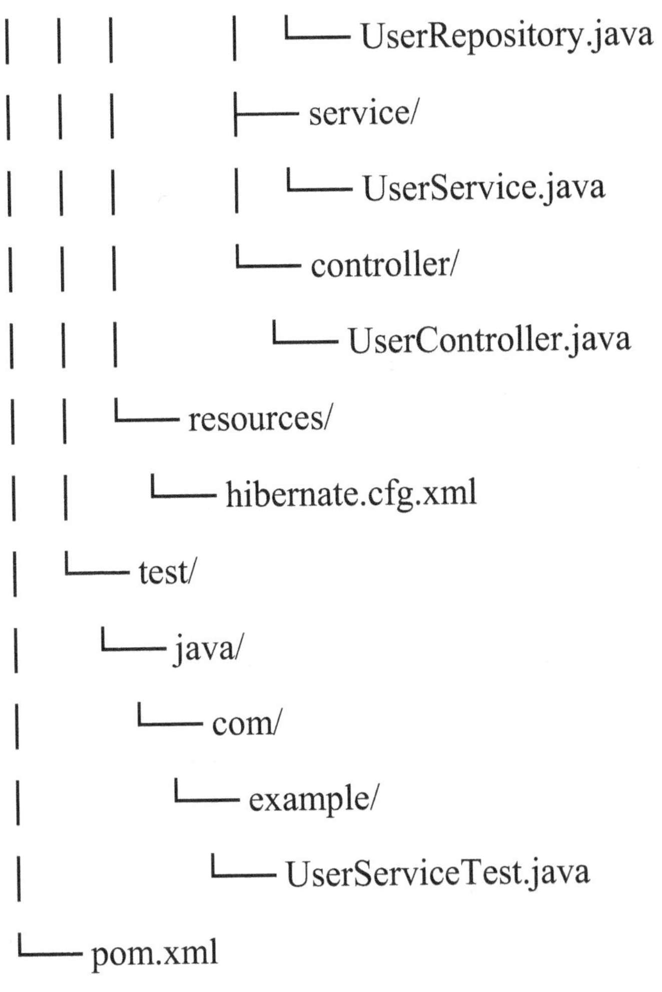

```
│   │   │           │   └── UserRepository.java
│   │   │           ├── service/
│   │   │           │   └── UserService.java
│   │   │           └── controller/
│   │   │               └── UserController.java
│   │   └── resources/
│   │       └── hibernate.cfg.xml
│   └── test/
│       └── java/
│           └── com/
│               └── example/
│                   └── UserServiceTest.java
└── pom.xml
```

1. Creating the `pom.xml` File

We start by creating a `pom.xml` file for the

Maven project. Let's ensure to include the necessary dependencies:

```xml
<project
xmlns="http://maven.apache.org/POM/4.0.0"

xmlns:xsi="http://www.w3.org/2001/XMLSchema-instance"

xsi:schemaLocation="http://maven.apache.org/POM/4.0.0
http://maven.apache.org/xsd/maven-4.0.0.xsd">

    <modelVersion>4.0.0</modelVersion>


    <groupId>com.example</groupId>

    <artifactId>hibernate-example</artifactId>

    <version>1.0-SNAPSHOT</version>


    <properties>
```

```
<hibernate.version>5.6.3.Final</hibernate.ver
sion>
      <spring.version>5.3.13</spring.version>
      <mysql.version>8.0.25</mysql.version>
      <junit.version>5.7.1</junit.version>
   </properties>

   <dependencies>
      <dependency>
         <groupId>org.hibernate</groupId>
         <artifactId>hibernate-core</artifactId>
         <version>$
{hibernate.version}</version>
      </dependency>
      <dependency>
         <groupId>org.hibernate</groupId>
         <artifactId>hibernate-
entitymanager</artifactId>
```

```
            <version>$
{hibernate.version}</version>
        </dependency>
        <dependency>
            <groupId>mysql</groupId>
            <artifactId>mysql-connector-
java</artifactId>
            <version>${mysql.version}</version>
        </dependency>
        <dependency>

<groupId>org.springframework</groupId>
            <artifactId>spring-context</artifactId>
            <version>${spring.version}</version>
        </dependency>
        <dependency>

<groupId>org.springframework</groupId>
            <artifactId>spring-orm</artifactId>
```

```
        <version>${spring.version}</version>
      </dependency>
      <dependency>
        <groupId>org.junit.jupiter</groupId>
        <artifactId>junit-jupiter-
engine</artifactId>
        <version>${junit.version}</version>
        <scope>test</scope>
      </dependency>
   </dependencies>

   <build>
      <plugins>
        <plugin>

<groupId>org.apache.maven.plugins</groupI
d>
            <artifactId>maven-compiler-
plugin</artifactId>
```

```
                <version>3.8.1</version>
                <configuration>
                    <source>1.8</source>
                    <target>1.8</target>
                </configuration>
            </plugin>
        </plugins>
    </build>
</project>
```

2. Creating the `hibernate.cfg.xml` Configuration File

Now let's create the Hibernate configuration file (`hibernate.cfg.xml`) in the `src/main/resources` folder. This file defines the database connection properties.

```xml
<?xml version="1.0" encoding="utf-8"?>
<!DOCTYPE hibernate-configuration PUBLIC
      "-//Hibernate/Hibernate Configuration DTD 3.0//EN"
      "http://www.hibernate.org/dtd/hibernate-configuration-3.0.dtd">
<hibernate-configuration>
   <session-factory>
      <!-- Database connection settings -->
      <property name="hibernate.connection.driver_class">com.mysql.cj.jdbc.Driver</property>
      <property name="hibernate.connection.url">jdbc:mysql://localhost:3306/your_database_name</property>
      <property name="hibernate.connection.username">your_username</property>
```

```
        <property
name="hibernate.connection.password">your
_password</property>


        <!-- JDBC connection pool settings -->

        <property
name="hibernate.c3p0.min_size">5</property
>

        <property
name="hibernate.c3p0.max_size">20</proper
ty>

        <property
name="hibernate.c3p0.timeout">300</propert
y>

        <property
name="hibernate.c3p0.max_statements">50</
property>

        <property
name="hibernate.c3p0.idle_test_period">3000
</property>


        <!-- SQL dialect -->
```

```
        <property name="hibernate.dialect">org.hibernate.dialect.MySQL5Dialect</property>

        <!-- Show SQL -->
        <property name="hibernate.show_sql">true</property>

        <!-- Automatic schema creation -->
        <property name="hibernate.hbm2ddl.auto">update</property>
    </session-factory>
</hibernate-configuration>
```

Be sure to replace `your_database_name`, `your_username`, and `your_password` with your actual values.

3. Creating the `User` Entity

Now let's create the `User` entity in the `entity` folder. This entity represents the `users` table in the database.

```java
package com.example.entity;


import javax.persistence.*;


@Entity
@Table(name = "users")
public class User {


    @Id
    @GeneratedValue(strategy =
GenerationType.IDENTITY)
    private Long id;
```

```
@Column(name = "name")
private String name;

@Column(name = "email")
private String email;

public User() {}

public User(String name, String email) {
    this.name = name;
    this.email = email;
}

public Long getId() {
    return id;
}
```

```
public void setId(Long id) {
    this.id = id;
}

public String getName() {
    return name;
}

public void setName(String name) {
    this.name = name;
}

public String getEmail() {
    return email;
}

public void setEmail(String email) {
    this.email = email;
```

```
    }
}
```

4. Creating the `UserRepository`

Now let's create the `UserRepository` in the `repository` folder. We'll use Hibernate to manage data access.

```java
package com.example.repository;

import com.example.entity.User;
import org.hibernate.Session;
import org.hibernate.SessionFactory;
import org.hibernate.Transaction;

import java.util.List;
```

```
public class UserRepository {

    private SessionFactory sessionFactory;

    public UserRepository(SessionFactory
sessionFactory) {
        this.sessionFactory = sessionFactory;
    }

    public void save(User user) {
        Transaction transaction = null;
        try (Session session =
sessionFactory.openSession()) {
            transaction =
session.beginTransaction();
            session.save(user);
            transaction.commit();
        } catch (Exception e) {
```

```
            if (transaction != null) {
                transaction.rollback();
            }
            e.printStackTrace();
        }
    }

    public User findById(Long id) {
        User user = null;
        try (Session session =
sessionFactory.openSession()) {
            user = session.get(User.class, id);
        } catch (Exception e) {
            e.printStackTrace();
        }
        return user;
    }
```

```
public List<User> findAll() {
    List<User> users = null;
    try (Session session =
sessionFactory.openSession()) {
        users = session.createQuery("from
User", User.class).list();
    } catch (Exception e) {
        e.printStackTrace();
    }
    return users;
}

public void update(User user) {
    Transaction transaction = null;
    try (Session session =
sessionFactory.openSession()) {
        transaction =
session.beginTransaction();
        session.update(user);
```

```
            transaction.commit();
        } catch (Exception e) {
            if (transaction != null) {
                transaction.rollback();
            }
            e.printStackTrace();
        }
    }

    public void delete(Long id) {
        Transaction transaction = null;
        try (Session session =
sessionFactory.openSession()) {
            transaction =
session.beginTransaction();
            User user = session.get(User.class, id);
            if (user != null) {
                session.delete(user);
            }
```

```
            transaction.commit();
        } catch (Exception e) {
            if (transaction != null)

   {
                transaction.rollback();
            }
            e.printStackTrace();
        }
    }
}
```

5. Creating `HibernateUtil` for SessionFactory Configuration

We need to create a utility class (`HibernateUtil`) to manage the `SessionFactory`.

```java
package com.example.config;

import org.hibernate.SessionFactory;
import org.hibernate.cfg.Configuration;

public class HibernateUtil {

    private static SessionFactory sessionFactory;

    public static SessionFactory getSessionFactory() {
        if (sessionFactory == null) {
            try {
                sessionFactory = new Configuration().configure().buildSessionFactory();
```

```
        } catch (Exception e) {
            e.printStackTrace();
        }
    }
    return sessionFactory;
  }
}
```

6. Creating the `UserService`

We will create the `UserService` to encapsulate business logic and interaction with the `UserRepository`.

```java
package com.example.service;

import com.example.entity.User;
```

```
import
com.example.repository.UserRepository;

import java.util.List;

public class UserService {

    private UserRepository userRepository;

    public UserService(UserRepository
userRepository) {
        this.userRepository = userRepository;
    }

    public void createUser(User user) {
        userRepository.save(user);
    }

    public User getUserById(Long id) {
```

```
        return userRepository.findById(id);
    }

    public List<User> getAllUsers() {
        return userRepository.findAll();
    }

    public void updateUser(User user) {
        userRepository.update(user);
    }

    public void deleteUser(Long id) {
        userRepository.delete(id);
    }
}
```

7. Creating the `UserController`

The `UserController` will act as the REST API controller.

```java
package com.example.controller;

import com.example.config.HibernateUtil;
import com.example.entity.User;
import com.example.repository.UserRepository;
import com.example.service.UserService;
import org.hibernate.SessionFactory;

import java.util.List;

public class UserController {

    private UserService userService;
```

```
public UserController() {
    SessionFactory sessionFactory =
HibernateUtil.getSessionFactory();
    userService = new UserService(new
UserRepository(sessionFactory));
}

public void createUser(String name, String
email) {
    userService.createUser(new User(name,
email));
}

public User getUserById(Long id) {
    return userService.getUserById(id);
}

public List<User> getAllUsers() {
```

```
        return userService.getAllUsers();
    }

    public void updateUser(Long id, String name, String email) {
        User user = userService.getUserById(id);
        user.setName(name);
        user.setEmail(email);
        userService.updateUser(user);
    }

    public void deleteUser(Long id) {
        userService.deleteUser(id);
    }
}
```

8. Testing with `UserServiceTest`

Finally, create unit tests to ensure functionality works as expected.

```java
package com.example;

import com.example.config.HibernateUtil;
import com.example.entity.User;
import com.example.repository.UserRepository;
import com.example.service.UserService;
import org.hibernate.SessionFactory;
import org.junit.jupiter.api.Test;

import static org.junit.jupiter.api.Assertions.assertEquals;
import static org.junit.jupiter.api.Assertions.assertNotNull;
```

```
public class UserServiceTest {

    private UserService userService;

    public UserServiceTest() {
        SessionFactory sessionFactory =
HibernateUtil.getSessionFactory();
        userService = new UserService(new
UserRepository(sessionFactory));
    }

    @Test
    public void testCreateUser() {
        User user = new User("John Doe",
"john.doe@example.com");
        userService.createUser(user);
        User savedUser =
userService.getUserById(user.getId());
```

```
        assertNotNull(savedUser);
        assertEquals("John Doe", savedUser.getName());
    }
}
```

This is a simple project structure to get started with Hibernate in a real-world application. You can build upon this base to include more advanced features such as complex relationships, validation, transaction management, and more.

9.Glossary of Hibernate

1. **Entity**

A Java object that represents a table in the database. Instances of the entity correspond to rows in the table.

2. **Persistent Object**

An object that has been saved to the database via Hibernate. Its state is synchronized with the database.

3. **Session**

An interface that represents a single unit of work with the database. It manages CRUD (Create, Read, Update, Delete) operations and transactions.

4. **SessionFactory**

An interface that represents a session factory. It creates Session objects and manages

Hibernate's configuration and settings.

5. **Transaction**

An interface representing a transaction in the context of Hibernate. It allows grouping multiple operations into a single atomic unit of work.

6. **Configuration**

The class used to configure Hibernate, including database connection details and mapping properties.

7. **Mapping**

The process of associating Java classes with database tables. This can be done via XML files or annotations.

8. **HQL (Hibernate Query Language)**

An object-oriented query language similar to

SQL, used to interact with the database through entities.

9. **Criteria API**

A programmatic API that allows building queries in a typed and object-oriented way, avoiding direct use of HQL.

10. **Named Query**

A statically defined query associated with an entity. It can be reused and optimized by the framework.

11. **Cache**

A mechanism that stores query results to reduce database access time. Hibernate supports two levels of cache: First-Level Cache and Second-Level Cache.

12. **First-Level Cache**

The default cache associated with a session. It

stores persistent objects for the duration of the session.

13. **Second-Level Cache**

A cache shared among sessions. It allows persistent objects to be stored even when they are no longer in the current session.

14. **Dirty Checking**

A mechanism in Hibernate that checks if an object has been modified during the session, and if necessary, synchronizes the changes with the database.

15. **Fetching Strategy**

A strategy that determines how and when data should be fetched from the database. It can be **Eager** (loads data immediately) or **Lazy** (loads data only when requested).

16. **Cascade**

A configuration that defines how operations on a parent entity affect associated entities. For example, if a parent entity is deleted, related entities can be deleted automatically.

17. **Association**

A relationship between two or more entities. Associations can be of different types: One-to-One, One-to-Many, Many-to-One, Many-to-Many.

18. **Inheritance**

A mechanism for handling class hierarchies in Hibernate, allowing the use of mapping strategies for entity inheritance.

19. **Composite Key**

A primary key made up of multiple columns. In Hibernate, it can be handled using a composite key class.

20. **EntityManager**

Part of the JPA (Java Persistence API), it represents the persistence context where entity operations occur.

21. **JPA (Java Persistence API)**

A standard interface for data persistence in Java, which can be used together with Hibernate as an implementation.

22. **Dialect**

A class that provides translation between Hibernate's query language (HQL) and the specific query language of the database being used.

23. **Schema Generation**

The process of automatically creating the database schema from mapped entities, which can occur in various modes: `create`, `update`, `validate`, `none`.

24. **Interceptor**

An object that can be used to intercept and modify the behavior of Hibernate operations, such as entity loading and saving.

25. **Event Listeners**

Mechanisms that allow responding to specific events in the entity lifecycle, such as saving or deleting.

26. **Batch Processing**

A technique that allows multiple operations to be executed in a single request to the database, improving performance.

27. **Projection**

A mechanism for retrieving only a subset of an entity's properties, rather than the entire object.

28. **Entity Graph**

A way to define which relationships of an entity should be fetched in a fetching operation.

29. **Validation**

The process of checking the validity of entities based on defined rules, which can occur via annotations or external configurations.

30. **Multi-tenancy**

A mechanism that allows handling multiple schemas or databases in a single application, useful in SaaS (Software as a Service) scenarios.

31. **Transaction Isolation Levels**

Levels that define the degree of visibility of transactions to each other in the database. Hibernate supports various isolation levels such as Read Uncommitted, Read Committed,

Repeatable Read, and Serializable.

This glossary provides a comprehensive overview of key terms and concepts in Hibernate. Understanding these terms is essential for working effectively with Hibernate and for developing robust and high-performance Java applications.

Index

www.ingramcontent.com/pod-product-compliance
Lightning Source LLC
Chambersburg PA
CBHW052152220526
45471CB00004B/1638